of love *and* drowning

of love *and* drowning

poems *1985–2008*

ANTONY CHRISTIE

Library and Archives Canada Cataloguing in Publication

Christie, Antony, 1943-
Of love and drowning : poems 1985-2008 / Antony Christie.
ISBN 978-1-55081-324-1
I. Title.
PS8605.H743O4 2010 C811'.6 C2010-900129-X

BREAKWATER BOOKS LTD. acknowledges the support of the Canada Council for the Arts which last year invested $1.3 million in the arts in Newfoundland. We acknowledge the financial support of the Government of Canada through the Book Publishing Industry Development Program for our publishing activities. We acknowledge the financial support of the Government of Newfoundland and Labrador through the department of Tourism, Culture and Recreation for our publishing activities.

Printed in Canada

Canada Council for the Arts Conseil des Arts du Canada

This book has been printed on 100% post consumer waste paper, certified Eco-logo and processed chlorine free.

A climbing moon upon an empty sky,
And all that lamentation of the leaves,
Could but compose man's image and his cry.

from W.B. Yeats: "The Sorrow of Love"

Contents

Of love and drowning

fault lines

Daybreak and a candle end.

from W.B.Yeats: "The Wild Wicked Old Man"

Living in the earthquake zone

i

the house is stone and mortar –
no compromise here –
the beams of squared pine
would snap the spine
at one twitch.
we have set the table
on the wide balcony,
take black tea and honey,
nibble at almond cakes.

ii

the tree by the church gate
has showered the cobbles
with berries.
the children from mass
stamp out a pool of black blood.
you drop marigold petals
one by one
into the abyss.
you smile.

iii

we eat bread and brown cheese
in the walled garden.
you have a plate of green olives.
a falcon comes suddenly

between the houses,
snatches a thrush
from under the stone bench.
before we can cry out
it is a bundle of dead feathers.

iv

today
we are climbing
between rough walls and goat bells
to the white top of the ridge.
sleet hits us full in the face.
I hold your hand more firmly,
have ceased to wonder
whether the sky is shaking or still,
expecting and not expecting the avalanche,
your face blurred and bloody
through the ice window.

green as

green as summer

Dance there upon the shore;
What need have you to care
For wind or water's roar?
And tumble out your hair
That the salt drops have wet;
Being young …

W.B. Yeats: "To a Child Dancing in the Wind"

First day

and so he came to a new country,
to a grey plain busier than
he could have imagined
where boys in coarse jackets and black boots
spoke a strange language and spat
and pale girls mothered him into a space
big as a barn.

there desks were set round a throne
where a grandmother with a ruler
beat time. he made marks
she said were his name on a grey slate
with chalk that squeaked and she told of
a man in a rainbow coat who was thrown
into a hole.

they gave him a grey dinner and made
him wee against a white wall.
then there were crayons and a coal fire,
now the day is over and mittens.
and after such a long, long journey
even the most familiar faces
were not safe.

Yard sale

last night you gathered your childhood
from under the bunkbed,
the attic,
the playhouse in the woodshed roof,
had laid it out before breakfast
on sheets of blue plastic
by the day lilies on the front lawn.

the signs are out on the highway
and soon you will have a fistful of dollars
and your first skis
and the barbie clothes
your mother made you before each Christmas
and your Dr. Seuss collection
will be making memories
for other parents to treasure.

when you are there,
childhood is a place to escape
as painlessly and quickly as you can,
though they hang snares in the kitchen
(me on a tricycle aged four)
and pass round baby photos
disguised as landscapes
that make your friends snicker.

Viewing the house

someone had stencilled the pink room
with red and purple flowers.
a pine bed with white sheets
waited for the daughter
who had followed stars over her slope of sky
as they shouted and shed tears.

it is a sad house, you said.
the paper had peeled in the damp,
glass cracked, as for three years
they could not even agree
on a price.

I knew the tides and changing hills
would be your view, the blue room.
I look northeast as she looked.
the candle trees burn in the high sun –
each evening the last light tints palely
the east side of the square.

below us the house is shifting,
taking our shape –
two chairs by a fire of peat and coal,
a table with a checked cloth,
a bowl of fruit.
there are sunflowers in a glazed pot
on the flags by the back door,
forgetmenots, wild pansies.

we would give her if we could
a new childhood to grow into
and through.

Saturday afternoon

red-kneed, he roughs in
grass and a blue sky –
the finishing touches.
the shoppers on Grafton Street
give barely a glance
at his chalk house
in pink and pale yellow –
tourists, occasional visitors
take a quick look
but give him nothing.

three doors away,
his sister, her dull hair tangled,
pink cardigan half open,
plays slow tunes
on a school recorder,
her stub fingers forcing strict time,
her begging bag also empty.

it is easier
to drop money
into the fiddle case
where Handel is being played, well,
in front of the Body Shop.

Almost a still life

the fat girl in royal blue lycra
tackles
head on
the same slow hill;
sweat chafes
her back and thighs –
the pedals turn,
just.

her more athletic friend
kneels in hot pink
by the bright red mountain bike
by the yellow pole
where an aluminum hasp snaps the electric fence
to a full circuit,
breaks as she waits
the blackened snags of sedge and golden rod
and Queen Anne's lace to smaller
and smaller
straws.

their object,
the horse in the wired pound
pulls philosophically
at greener grass
as the shingled barn sheds, imperceptibly,
its tarnished ridge
of pale distorted worlds.

The new tenants

they have told us we can walk under the apple trees,
they remember your father.
'it was sad,' they tell me,
'the way he went down so quickly.'

we open the orchard gate he welded
from a bedframe and iron fence posts,
a classic improvization.
brown and white cattle graze carelessly on windfalls,
hens scratch for grubs
and you tell me of the games you played here,
show me the scar on your left arm that needed nine stitches,
seem five or six as you lift your dress
to scratch the mosquito bite on your right thigh.

you make me see the geese he kept here,
more reliable than guard dogs,
tastier than turkey at Christmas and Thanksgiving,
the rabbits, your favourites, in neat white hutches.
you pick a green grey sturmer from a low branch,
polish it on your jeans jacket,
smile as you fold my hand round the firm flesh,
tell me to bite.

'I was twelve,'
you tell me to my face then,
quietly,
too calmly,
as we chew the sweet flesh.
'we were picking the last trees.
he was drunk already, often,
though not ill,
not yet.'

when we reach the highway
you have almost straightened your face.
'I will write to them,' you say, 'thank them,
say I'm sorry we didn't stop for tea and muffins.'

chickadees are singing, the sky, again, is fall yellow,
the air brittle with the promise of frost.
I squeeze your hand, gently, quite out of my depth.

Bricks

that was the year we built the fort
of bricks and round stones
on the rocks near Webster's Point
when the ice went out.
all spring we roasted marshmallows on driftwood fires,
squashed June bugs,
hunted Indians and tree frogs among the dwarf willows.
we fought the War of 1812 again and again
along the curved beach,
repulsed Americans and mad French
and in the hiatus between grade eight and high school
went skinnydipping under the fierce stars
though we were shy of our new bodies
or took the Webers' canoe as far as we dared
out onto the silver lake.
it was there we caught what might have been
a flayed porcupine or a blind puppy but wasn't.
later the OPP took away
Matt Hoffmayer's sister and then his father.
before Labour Day
we kicked the fort to pieces
brick by brick.
it was the least we could do.

Fourteen

she has marked
her mouth
with a red O
scored it on thick
made a hard mask of it
in case
that stirring and fluttering
that is not
at all like indigestion
would make
her real lips
tremble
and say yes
yes
far too soon.

Fiction

it was already November
and the creekbank behind the bleachers
at the edge of Confederation Park
had lost its appeal.
it seemed we had squandered
the whole of our first summer
until the hydro shorted
in the first flurry of new snow
and ten minutes of the purest night
as thick and bittersweet as treacle
glued us irrevocably together
at least for the winter
and part of the next spring
(we were only fifteen)
though FICTION must be
the least auspicious place
to begin.

Green as summer

two girls on a pink rock,
the sun at midmorning.
the lake is
green as summer.

lovers or friends?
certainly their physicality
is striking –
the fair one spread on a towel,

the dark one sitting so straight
under her wide white hat,
as she writes
in her blue, hand-covered

hard-bound notebook –
poetry it must be –
for the world?
for her chosen audience of one?

two luminous blue dragonflies
joined head to tail
heedlessly
skim the near water.

Language barrier

you had too many tears
for your fingers to hold in,
they had made snail tracks
over your hands
and damp patches
around your buttoned wrists.

I wanted to talk to you,
perhaps to hold you,
to say the words
that would open you
to the night sky
and make you smile,

but being able only
to count to two,
say please and thank you and hi
and ask for coffee or beer
I felt impossibly
ill-equipped,

so you did not see
the first stars,
and made no wish
(if wishes are made
in Finnish or Estonian
on the last boat from Tallinn).

caliban's island

'I am King of the Peacocks,'

from W.B. Yeats: "A Man Young and Old"

Prospero's arrival

I was snaring mullet
when a grey bird
with ghosts riding her back
blew in with the late tide.

I covered my flesh
as I had been taught
smeared red clay
on my cheeks and palms.

he spoke to me in a language of his own,
the old ghost,
made wild signs with his hands.
I cowered.

his brow was like the sun,
his eyes blue as the sea.
I trembled as I called him
father.

Child's play

his child named me Bucephalus.
she sat on my dark haunches,
threaded me a halter of copper
and glass beads.

when she clapped her hands,
I carried her
where the water was sweetest,
found her raspberries and wild honey.
I ate her father's food.

I squandered
my mother's knowledge
for a steel knife
and a blanket,
for human voices.

Caliban in love

I watch all night
in a crook of rock and white birch,
keep from her
the shadows of night birds.

her flesh is
the bloom of wild apples,
she is straight as water.

if I swallow my breath,
I can hear her eyes moving
under their lids,
smell her salt blood.

I will trace with my tongue
the folds of her arms and back;
we will make giants together.

Hangover

their fire burnt my throat
sweetly.

the fume of it in my eyes
twisted the tall pines till they danced,
turned the stars
in a great tidepool of black water.

wings beat at me like lungs.
the rock fell from under me;
the air I swam in
was thick as sand.

she would take me now,
now I was a god.

her father set hornets on them
and they cowered like slow apes,
writhed crazily in the hot sand.
for my error,
he took her back to the sea.

I lap swamp water like a dog,
chew twigs and dry berries,
tear limbs from lizards and sour toads.
I smear my legs with the dung of wild pigs.

if I become what he made me
I can be free of her.

Much later: another ship

it is, as you suspected,
an island.
what more do you want?

perhaps,
like those who came before you,
a speck of green in the far emptiness
of ocean
brittle as a mirage
lured you to extravagant preconceptions.

an island is neutral,
it will take the form it is given –
paradise or absence,
your choice.

so the gnarled limestone is a disappointment,
the sharp juniper scrub,
the thorns that slash your fine clothing.
they will bear berries,
grudgingly, not at this season,

you do not care to gnaw the bones
of squirrels and small birds?
there are others.

# of love and drowning

Dread has followed longing,

And our hearts are torn.

from W.B. Yeats: "Love's Loneliness"

Mirror image

through a thin smoke
of crickets and seed feathers
you ran from me over the headland
between the thorns
snapping the brittle grass,
the sky yellow and heavy,
the water so still –
the white cliffs were sky high, sea deep,
which real? which mirror?
and the steel eyes on your dress
flickered with caught fire
as we watched the storm build
over the mainland hills
and I held your body
close against my body,
such a good fit.

Keepsake

after we made love
for the first time
you took off your clothes
and folded them
into a neat pile,
and gave me
the silver chain
I mended with a paper clip
to hold
until morning.

I said
I still did not know
the right words
and begged you
to wait with me
at least until autumn
but you kissed me gently
between the eyes
and slid like an otter
into the dark pool.

Aubade

sometimes I bring a new poem,
once flowers,
more often nothing but myself
to the table you have set for me
in your square kitchen
before the sun rises
golden or thin yellow over the flat marsh.

I eat what you offer,
toast, honey, fresh fruit,
savour the coarse sweetness of coffee
you brew in a steel jug.
thus we have made a ritual of compromise,
feeling and breathing the essence
of each other with few significant words.

we have come so far now
the future no longer seems impossible.

You are sitting

you are sitting very quietly
by the screen door
watching two chipmunks
scatter a drift of fall leaves
the snow has drained of colour.

the creek is heavy
with mud and meltwater.

the tree frogs are not yet singing.

soon I will bring you
fireflies
and the hummingbird with the red throat
and you will stand in meadows
blazing with hawkweed
beside the blue lake.

This is not a photograph of you

if the smaller figure
standing by the low trees
in a strange garden
is your daughter
she has certainly aged,
I could not tell it was her.
the older is more familiar –
that same colour of hair,
that shape of chin and mouth,
but it is not you.
I have not touched the scars
on that body,
its voice has not
cut holes in me.
I would not kiss that stranger's lips
in the open street.

Houseboat in winter

I rise before dawn,
construct a careful pyramid
of damp coal.
the stove splutters,
leaks smoke,
grudgingly coaxes
towards blood heat
the kettle of black tea.

ice nudges the hull
a plank's width from your ear –
you shift, make words in your sleep,
draw the quilt tighter, settle.
I thumb through yesterday's paper
waiting for you to wake.
the bread is cut and buttered,
the milk in the cup.
I have wiped the oilcloth clean.

Working lunch

take that soft look
off your face,
the distance out of your eyes,
drain that colour
from your cheeks –
put on your clothes
and we'll have a beer,
talk seriously about
feminism
and the poetry of Christina Rossetti,
make ourselves
professionally fit
for the long
slow
tedious
afternoon.

Prinsenhof sequence: Amsterdam, April 1998

1. Evening flight

through gusts of rain and thin cloud
our squat aluminum 737
peels off the last layers of light,
climbs eastward.
my skin loosens –
I am shedding the relics of sour talk,
the paw prints of failed intimacy;
already we are painting
rows of loud tulips onto the dark fields
as we study the intricacies of water and bridges,
the shapes of gables,
the mysteries of the strippenkaart.

2. Arrival

of course we guessed the wrong tram,
had to carry our full rucksacks a whole kilometre
over arched bridges, along quays under construction,
past trees hung with green coins,
but we found the message,
exchanged it for envelope and key,
mastered the double door
and were in.

we had imagined a canal view,
water and a flat façade,
but not the room itself,
so the long space that drew us
past washplace, wardrobe, cane table and chairs
to the wide bed by the window
under the beams and the angle of wall and roof
was at once a surprise and a delight,
a place recognized and acknowledged.
it was a homecoming and a beginning –
even the roofscape was right,
the patio fenced with the ghost stalks of summer
under a searing moon.

3. Sunday, early

the first light seeps
around and through
the green cotton of your spring duvet.
you are lying on your left side,
your eyes half open.
you stretch and arch your back
as I trace with fingertips and tongue
your creases and mounds,
your new curves.

4. Museums

i. Rembrandt

the effrontery of the man
to paint his own dissolution into an apostle –
this St. Paul of his
has had far too much genever.
no wonder the honest burghers shunned him.
better his shy, shadowed self-depreciation
before he grew that ostentatious moustache
or learnt to hold his head at a rakish angle.

ii. Van Gogh

his dark palette was for peasants and potatoes.
later there were sunflowers and irises,
a brother's love,
the bedroom he painted twice –
cane chair and washstand,
the coats hanging,
the red blanket on the pine bed,
the pictures staring,
at what?
when he shot himself in the chest
he took two days to die;
crows in a wheatfield –
the track leads nowhere.

iii. The others

Anne Frank and the History of Marijuana?
the Museum of Naval Architecture?
forget it.

5. Shopping

among the cannabis seeds
whose merits the young assistant
was so eager to explain,
the smoking pipes,
the porno videos
whose price stickers hide
wide open cunts
or pricks angled for instant entry
in all shapes and colours
we were foolish to dream of
silver rings in two days.
but I have bought you a carrier bag
of fifty tulips,
blood from a fresh cut,
so you can fill all your vases with longing
and you have a tee shirt for your son,
a stoned Van Gogh,
to play to that part of our stereotype
that is safe for older children.

6. Ristorante Caprese

she brought us back too suddenly
from wherever it was we were,
hands linked on the table,
deep in each other,
by asking us if we wanted dessert,
and to cover the general embarrassment
we unconvincingly pretended
we were watching the traffic police
wheel clamp a German BMW.

7. *Night walk*

beyond the shuttered flower market,
the smoking coffee houses,
the edge of porn country
we concertina walk the night canal ring
under the dripping elms.

tonight they have hung out their kitchens,
their parlours and offices,
sit alone or in family groups,
with or without dog,
child,
wine glass,
coffee cup,
a moving gallery
behind reflecting windows and floating gardens.

a serious audience,
we weigh
the merits of flat or houseboat
as if we had
our first apartment to rent.

8. Still life: nude

the next time I opened my eyes
you were leaning out between the curtains
framed and completely still.
the low sun
edged your body in clean yellow,
an aura, a halo,
a capsule of clear amber.

that moment was ten years long
when you turned to me
your face still bright with morning,
your hair tangled
in the blue of the new sky.

9. Lessons to be learnt

you are better with left and right
and with passports,
but I can handle north and south
which is more useful
for catching trams.

you must limit museums
to two or three hours a day –
the rest spend walking by canals,
in cafés,
browsing the flower stalls
or watching coots.

the trees are, of course,
dutch elms.

we like individual duvets
on a double mattress,
a room under the eaves,
eggs and sliced cheese for breakfast,
the coffee.

you *can* have an orgasm
after you've been drinking
on and off all day,
but it takes time
and a number of different,
careful, approaches.

I will still make love with you
if you shave off
all your hair.

10. Homecoming

I have left you, as you asked,
at the green wicket gate,
your face broken.

it is almost too hard now
to fit back into the slots we find necessary,
to make the right noises,
but there are gardens and half built walls,
though these have dangers of their own,
there are children unwinding the flesh cords
that keep the heart distant,
the whole web of family.

the tulips with blood petals
are staring at you accusingly from an army of vases –
your flask has laid an ambush under my car seat.

in June the elms along Prinsengracht will be in green leaf,
the eggs in the coot's nest of cans, twigs, styrofoam and paper
against the rudder of the next to last houseboat
will have ripened to black fruit
that move like puppets on the brown water.
the sun will be shining in a sky of tiles.

Absence

I have plumped two pillows
smoothed the sheets
put out your glass of milk and water
fixed the light so it will not shine in my eyes
if you read yourself to sleep.
and if I keep to my side of the bed
and do not reach tentatively for you
from an unquiet dream
or wake too slowly at first light
and turn to you as I do
on more fortunate mornings
I will keep you all night a breathing space away
and with no sense of absurdity
will make two cups of coffee
heat two croissants in the temperamental gas oven
lay two places at the breakfast table.

In Zoraya's garden

The Patio de los Cipreses in the Alhambra palace, Granada, Spain, where Zoraya, wife of Sultan Abu'I Hassan, and her lover Hamet were found together in a hollow cypress tree.

the plane leaves fall slowly in the dry heat,
the fountains are all on fire,
even the alley cats
in the passages behind the new cathedral
are sleeping.

when the blind sun
drives me to shade and water
in the slow hours after mid day
I miss particularly your scars,
the sharp imperfections of your body,
the mole under your left breast,
the age lines on your chin,
and your voice, your voice above all things.

if you were with me now I would love you for ever.
if you were with me now the lotus and the lion
would shed glad tears for us
in Zoraya's garden under the hollow cypress
where Hamet braided her hair with gold and silver beads
with thread the colour of kisses and red blood
under the white and the pink oleander,
under the rose, under the orange hibiscus.

Small packet from Greece

a bougainvillea
quite unexpectedly
in the first pages of your book.

its petals are paper too,
pink-purple,
the perfect stamens
clouded
with moon yellow seed.

here the goldenrod
is fall ragged,
the maples bloody edged,
brittle.
bears wander close in
stuffing their fat
with blueberries and slow frogs.

it will be dawn soon
under the walnut trees
by the blue sea.
the fishermen
are spreading their nets.

When

when I came down
from the mountains
it was late summer.
the buddleia shed
butterflies and drunk bees
and the marigolds
were burning.

I came without ceremony
over the threshold
between the scrubbed shelves
to the cold hearth
where flies danced
in the chimney light,
where you were waiting.

I had brought you seeds,
and honey in a stone jar,
but you drew from me
words not meant
to be spoken
and the sweetness
had leached from your eyes.

It is full summer

and I had not noticed.

the soil crumbles like dark bread –
too early to name
those small pillows of plump greenness
pumpkin or sunflower, and is that
rye grass or spears of young corn?

the lilacs have withered already,
camellias string blood gouts over the south wall,
the sweetness of tongued honeysuckle
numbs
the slow bees.

pink roses are whispering,
love?
          love?

the creek is warm enough
to drown in.

Night in July

you have brought out
a bowl of fresh fruit.

I stick my thumb
under the loose skin,
peel back the pith.
I loosen the segments.
juice
bursts in my face.
my eyes water.

and we sit,
swallowing the sweet flesh,
on the screen porch
in the hard heat,
feigning indifference.
it is a pose
we have honed
to a fine art.

soon we will be able
to tell
our children:
yes,
it was always
like this.

Buying the island

was your idea,
last fall, when the maples were
(of course)
red-orange
and green lights grew in the north sky.

in the first sharp mornings
careless of clothes and conversation
we threw off the quilt
and probed with words and tongue
the texture of new maps –

now, caught in the silence of stoves,
there is too much light –
the ice is treacherous,
currents scrape at it, make pittraps,
hide them with new snow.

we look at each other with teeth,
draw in our blankets
like the ghosts of the old nations.
we have discovered
how easy it is to crave raw food.

Falling into the night

it is no longer raining.

I am weeding the lower bed,
the one by the dyke
where marigolds are deep yellow.
my hands
are grained with cold earth.
there are docks and two-inch nettles
in my near vision.
I am blinking the midges
from eyes that have learnt
not to make tears.

this is not what I wanted to say.

if you were here,
I would hold you.
you would be able to find
the right words.

Hiatus

you come into a room
you think you should know well
though you no longer remember why.
you heap logs on the open stove.
the cat purrs at you,
you scratch her behind the ears.
automatically you stuff the winter quilt
into the blue and white striped cover,
half draw the blinds,
put out a clean towel.

the sky is burning gold and deep purple.
soon the full moon
will silhouette the bare maples.
as you listen for
the sound of her brown boots
you notice for the first time
the bare stalks in the green vase,
the drift of rose petals,
the page marked with that cancelled ticket
from the La Spezia bus.

sometimes you are afraid
you are forgetting how to breathe.

And today

is the right sort of a day for planting plaques.
you are wearing funereal black
(because of the weather, you tell me, it's not meant
    to be symbolic)
as we climb the steep track from
HERE WE SAW THE FIRST LAKE DISTRICT LLAMA
to
HERE I TOOK THE PHOTO THAT DIDN'T COME OUT
    ABOUT WHICH I WROTE THE POEM
    THAT WAS NEVER PUBLISHED.
it was earlier in the afternoon
but the sky was grey then, too, the bracken fall brown,
black pools in the ruts.
today it's dark soon after
HERE I KICKED THE GOOSE AND WAS SET UPON
    BY THE GAY PAINTER
and we stumble back to the car along the rough path
    below the scree,
set feet in mud,
are not quite sure of the slope on the last hill before the Duddon.
so we miss
HERE YOU WANTED TO MAKE LOVE TO ME.
again.

And here we are

sitting on the sea wall
eating our nougat wafers
and playing at old friends.

we do it quite well these days,
share holidays and gardens,
trade stories of the children
with the right level of involvement,
laugh at the idiosyncrasies
of parents and partners,

though my role falters
as I walk through the opening garlic
in the wood at the bay's end
worrying about your cough,
your inconclusive tests,
the way the colour is draining
from your eyes.

two sisters on the beach
play sisters with passionate intensity,
hopscotching through the shallows
just wildly enough to splash intentionally
without being confrontational.
they have it to a tee.

some day I will learn to play our game
with more conviction.

The beach by Sea Wood

how did she ever talk me
into buying a dog?
this is the second,
the one she left me with,
white-yellow, part labrador.
they're faithful, she told me.
I like to think it was well meant.

usually I call her *dog*.
sometimes *cow*,
pig-ugly, *albatross*,
but even when she drips blood
it is not her fault.
this winter we are reclaiming, slowly,
the places she took from me.

this is the beach;
I have not been here for two years.
the spring tides have worried
the sand spit,
half buried the reeds
in kelp and raw plastic.
this time I crush the pink clam shells

under my boots.
now she has brought me a bone
from an old boat.
I am to throw it into the sea for her,
she understands this much.
fetch, I shout,
just like a professional.

Junk

your photograph,
back view of course;
behind, a red-brick church,
improbably blue sky.

it was, once.

a stone white virgin
opens her arms to you
over the picnic table,
the half-dead roses.

one more for the bin bag.

on second thoughts
I'll bluetack it to the wall
above my desk.
a warning.

Of love and drowning

i

see a ghost once
and you are done for.
they are trickier than twilight,
than edge vision,
impossible to laugh at.

ii

kiss a ghost on the lips
and it sucks the warmth out of you.
your skin crumbles like sand.
you have the ribs of a gull.

flies scrabble
for the dry scraps of your heart
but will not tear out of you
the black stone at the centre.

if a ghost kisses you
on the lips
it will eat even the black stone.

iii

to exorcise your ghost
you must climb to the shrine of the virgin
at the top of the blue pass,
carry the stone in your hand,
lay it on the ground
with all the others.
turn your back on it if you can.

if you pray to her
she will tell you
that haunting is better
than a cold bed.

iv

you have come back to the lake,
the long lake where you played
children and lovers
and the loon cry was not for you.
mists track like cottongrass,
milkweed, the ice trail of a silent jet.
the water is the colour of your eyes.

you are floating on your back now,
just below the surface.
your mouth is open.
the evening star has pierced
your white throat.

picking bones

All know that all the dead in the world about
that place are stuck,

And that should mother seek her son
she'd have but little luck

Because the fires of Purgatory have ate
their shapes away;

from W.B.Yeats: "The Pilgrim"

Sandy's mare

today you are grazing
the top pasture
beyond the grey scree
close to the sky.
the first snow is lying,
lightly.

it is a month now
since we met by chance
at the end of summer
your owner, our neighbour,
by the road gate
amongst harebells and hawkweed,
and you stretched towards her hand
and she told us, yes,
she was feeling much better
and yes, she would soon be walking
without a stick.

you are growing, with foal,
more noticeably round.
it will be born in the spring,
your second.
your first died at five days
last April in the black rain.
do you remember how she spoke to you then
and touched you, softly?

on Monday they will put her
into the ground
in the churchyard
by the low river
where the trees shed
dry tears
after the first frost
and the flowers have withered.

The road from Moffat

the young doe fell suddenly
from grace
on the high road
from Moffat into Tweeddale
where the forest hugs
both sides of a sharp bend.

the impact broke both her hind legs
but there was surprisingly
little blood.
we stopped the car
and saw at once
that the sharp bone had sliced
through muscle and skin,
knew we could do
nothing for her,

so we stood
guiltily undamaged,
only one headlight broken
and a dent in the door
on the driver's side,
listened to the rhythm
of her interminable breathing
as the autumn twilight
stretched out
in terrified incomprehension,
though it was less than a minute,

I think,
before she quivered and lay still
and we heard lark song
and the falling of distant water.

Love tokens

you have brought me
a strange corpse,
have laid it carefully
in the hollow left by my head.

it is a sleek russet,
its fierce eyes not yet glazed,
fifteen centimetres
from its dry black nose
to the black tip of its tail –
and feel those needle teeth!
a least weasel, and quite rare.
not that that did it any good.

it makes a change,
I suppose,
from the usual succession
of mice (jumping or deer),
field voles,
the occasional star-nosed mole.

and chipmunks –
they play dead,
scuttle off once your back is turned,
live under the bookshelves
for weeks,
smell worse than shrews.

and once
it was a red-bellied snake,
its gut slit,
trailing pale worms of intestines
over the quilt.

you sat and purred.

I finished that off with an axe,
buried it with the others
in the soft earth under the lilacs,
an offering some enterprising archaeologist
may some day
turn into a cult.

Plague pit

(not the year of the rabbit)

I am digging a plague pit
under the sycamores
by the far dyke.
the wet summer festers.

they are too many to ignore.
the sick that can still see cower
in the riot of herb robert
that all but covers the moist flags,

once I would crush their skulls
with a flat rock
as if I could kill pain.
I have lost that knack.

a few days and they will be
loud and stinking;
I will probe with a lawn rake,
penitent, cover my face

as I ease out limbs and skin
in one piece.
over the husks of bluebells,
the raw earth aches black and ready.

Picking bones

I am climbing the fell
to pick bones.

past the grey scree,
the furrowed firestone ledges,
by a black pool
opaque and frost pocked,
crusted with spring ice,
there is a wet patch of
green moss and pale juncus.
here, two winters ago,
a ewe died in a storm.

the peat has crumbled.
her fleece hid the sun
till flies and crows had done
their work in it.
last autumn, the spine
was one piece,
ligaments and gristle
glistened after the rain.
the ants were still busy.

now, bending, I scrape
a drift of frozen snow
from the smooth of the pelvis,
find the vertebrae
scattered, half buried,
smooth white.

this is what I was waiting for:
bone and horn –
here I am lucky too –
will shape and polish,
become gems,
move
to a different breathing.

My aunt's garden

my aunt is dying of bone cancer.

she moves meticulously
within a body
that is falling in on itself,
afraid of dissolution.

she is not old.

I put her tray of herbs
into the sun for her.
soon there will be green shoots.
her tulips are over,
but the grape hyacinths
are in full flower,
the bluebells luxuriate
and yellow and red blooms
I have no name for
pattern the flagged path.
the pear is in white blossom
against the north wall.

this is all a part of her.

her body is no longer friendly:
it must be kept at bay
with morphia
that makes her words slurred.

her garden is growing.

Italian grandmother

if you go camping,
take an Italian grandmother.
there is one just across the site.
each morning I see her sweeping the groundsheet
polishing handles and windows
before the family is up.
she smiles me *buon giorno*
as I cross to the shower block.

yesterday, before noon, under the pineta
where the cicadas were in full song
and martins and swallows
picked them from the high branches,
I saw her wobbling on a camp bicycle,
fresh bread in a white plastic bag
slung from each handlebar,
her face in the same smile,
and in the early evening
she was preparing salad in a red plastic bowl
on a white plastic picnic table
under the swept awning.

I wonder where she goes at night,
for there seems little room
in the aluminum and plastic trailer from Verona –
perhaps they have a basket for her
in the neat vegetable and pasta tent
at the end of the groundsheet piazza
where she can watch over her family
and rise with a smile
when the cicadas begin to sing.

Endgame

this is a game
to be played on fine spring mornings
outside the grocery store
whilst the thin-haired wives
are wrestling with wire baskets
and coins that have grown too small –

it is called 'making it safe,'
this liturgical spare us,
spare us just a little longer,
this pecking at the edges of the unspeakable
in a faltering recitation
of symptom and slow cure –

listen how those scarecrow gullets rattle
as the old men lay bare
their strokes and prostate operations
and the ravens cackle.

Or lilies?

when he was old enough
to know no better
he started to cry again at parting trains
and buy red roses.

something to do, he thought,
with a year he made love only once
at a pull-in on the old road while trucks thundered
across a strip of grey field.

his thumbs
are still fumbling
for the snap fasteners
between her legs.

My father is missing

he has taken his brown trilby
from the hatstand in the hall,
his beige coat with the patched lining,
chosen his best stick
and headed out up the paved track
working his legs like pistons
to keep strict time with his heart's
too finite residue of beating.

this is the way of things now –
while my mother spreads bounty from purpled hands
under the walnut tree they have tended for forty years
till the pigeons fall like vultures from the smeared tiles,
my father is going home,
at least as far as the highway
whose pace and roar
will stop him in his tracks.

soon it will be time to fetch him gently back,
to feed him the round red pills that glaze and settle,
take him some other where.

Family business

your turn to diaper father, I say,
shrinking from a second close contact
in two hours.

he squirms and whimpers,
searches the colour shapes of morning
with the blank eyes of a newborn
as you strip off the minimally soiled sheets,
lay starkly and shockingly bare
the thumb stub of our generation.

you powder and smear white cream
on a red welt which might prove ulcerous.
he chuckles. I catch a slight stirring
in the polyps of dead flesh, far underwater,
which, unembarrassed, you drown deftly
in folds of white cotton.

I hold up his head while he swallows
the ration of chemicals
that keeps him tranquil.

you stir the soup.

My mother in the visiting room

when her heart split,
this was what she became.

after the first shock
it is easier to understand
why they did not
bind her chin,
though the open mouth
mirrors too poignantly
her birth-damaged cousin
and she would never have been seen
in public
without her teeth.

they could not have known.

fish on a slab?
rag doll?
metaphors to trivialize
the unutterable,

the ultimate
o.

Clearing the house

we became methodical locusts
moving from room to room
stripping the cupboards of ornaments
and old china, what was left
of the blue-checked utility dinner service,
of boxes of negatives
clouded like cataract eyes
not seeing some distant summer
there was no-one left to remember –

now it was time for us to empty the toybox,
to open old wounds
(who was it drew circles in blue pen
on the doll with freckles and a red skirt?
who cut the lion's woollen mane?)
to promise, once this was all boxed
and consigned to the charities she had named
to meet at Christmas, next summer
the year after

children for this one last
not golden afternoon, we hid from each other
our own necessary relics: mine
the golly with the faded face
(made by a neighbour
from a wartime black stocking and an old red blouse)
my only companion that long sick spring
I lay in my grandmother's huge bed
and first dreamt of dying.

Playing god

the cat is dead too,
a quick uncomplicated glazing over
on the golden leaves
as I play god
and the kind vet with the needle
is an archangel
in the Indian summer garden.

this role becomes more treacherous
with each repetition –
I enter too soon, or too late,
or so I tell myself,
having no yardstick for feline suffering,
rehearsing perhaps too consciously
my own timed exit,
the hardest to perfect.

the blackbird that flew unseen
into the red sun
has broken its neck,
careless of god or angel,
without applause,
a limp rag on the bare earth
under the kitchen window.

Relics

new ice
has stubbed with glass gloves
the fine fingers of sweet cicely,
numbed the sharp
suppleness
of thistle and grass,
and now the false sun
is yellowing
their dead skin,
my father and mother,
damp with the spit beads
of our last live kisses.

Bargain basement
St. Michan's Church, Dublin

it was most like leather,
worn leather,
the arm of a chair,
the binding of a family bible.

'give her another feel,'
the guide said.
'you'll never do that again,
to a nun.'

we ran our fingers
obediently
over the shrunken ribcage
the colour of beer,
decorously keeping our distance,
though there was no chance
of arousing this nipple.

'how old?'
'five hundred if she's a day.'

so grey
with dust and cobwebs
save where our hands
had rubbed her
she could have been stone
or alabaster,

her head a formal death mask
save for the black lips
and tatters of rank hair,
her legs seamlessly
laced to her shrunk belly,
no sign of sex,

she had been carefully chosen,
this bride of christ,
laid out to be sensational
but not too shocking.

later, I read
she was probably
an eighteenth century fishwife.
whatever,
she would have made
a good pair of shoes.

A wet afternoon in the catacombs

look!
some eighteenth century joker
has made a love heart
out of skulls,
dreaming on the job
his own nightly resurrection
from under the streets of Paris.

was he desirable,
sought after,
fought over,
this carrier of bones?

it was a job for life,
emptying the graveyards,
the ossuaries,
democratically stacking
philosopher and leper
skull to skull.

was he a better lover
carrying between her sheets
the scent of bone dust?

Sea burial

when she stepped into the boat
she held the urn in her left hand.

the young man
laid a blue cloth over her seat,
took up the oars.

this was the best time, she thought:
though there was oil on the water,
and a dead fish, belly up, floated
with the wrack and ubiquitous plastic,
the mist hung close enough to mask
the bulk of tankers
and Russian factory ships that processed pilchards.

at the mouth of the bay
where the swell met them
red floats
still marked the nets and lobster pots –
she stood
and scattered them then
as her father had begged.

when she turned into the new sun
the young man
had spread the cloth on the planks
between the white seats –
she had known this all along,
stretched out her body to him
as he loosed with deft fingers
the gold buttons on her skirt.

sunday

sunday afternoon

Bid imagination run
Much on the Great Questioner;

from W.B.Yeats: "At Algeciras – A Meditation upon Death"

Talking with Becky by the river

she said
she would be eight
on Saturday
and asked how old I was

I told her

she thought about it
for a skip and two steps
and then said
that was old

and asked me
if I wasn't
scared of dying
as I would be dead soon

I asked her
if she was scared
and she said
yes

very

and picked
a blade of green grass
and asked me
to show her again
how to make it scream

Acknowledgements

The quotations on page 5, 11, 15, 31, 39, 75 and 101 are from *The Collected Poems of W.B.Yeats* (second edition). London, England: Macmillan and Company Ltd., 1950.

Some of the poems have been previously published in a chapbook:

"First day," "Night in July," Picking bones" and "Sandy's mare" in *Double Time*. Askam-in-Furness: Tidefall Press, 1994.

in anthologies:

"Saturday afternoon," "Italian grandmother" and "Road from Moffat" in *Aftermaths*. Barrow-in-Furness: Barrow Writers, 1995.

"It is full summer" in *Miracles and Clockwork*. Newcastle upon Tyne: Other Poetry, 2006.

"Viewing the house" was a prizewinner in the Lancaster Litfest, 1998, and appeared in *Litfest Poems 21*, the anthology published in Lancaster by Litfest.

and in the following magazines:

The Antigonish Review, Cobweb, Doors, Envoi, Fat Chance, Grain, Headlock, Orbis, Other Poetry, Pennine Platform, Poetry Ireland Review, Pottersfield Portfolio, Smiths Knoll, and Tandem.

www.ingramcontent.com/pod-product-compliance
Ingram Content Group UK Ltd.
Pitfield, Milton Keynes, MK11 3LW, UK
UKHW041820200726
13854UKWH00001BA/137

9 781550 813241